30 Day Whole F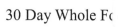

Whole Food: 30 Day Whole Food Challenge

AWARD WINNING Recipes for health, rapid weight loss, energy, detox, and food freedom GUARANTEED – Complete whole food 30 day diet cookbook meal plan

Albert Pino

30 Day Whole Food Challenge

Legal notice

This book is copyright (c) 2016 by Albert Pino. All rights reserved. This book may not be copied or duplicated in whole or in part via any means including electronic forms of duplication such as audio or video recording or transcription. The contents of this book may not be stored in any retrieval system, transmitted, or otherwise copied for any use whether public or private, other than brief quotations contained in articles or reviews which fall under the "fair use" exception, without express prior permission of the publisher.

This book provides information only. The author does not offer any advice, medical or otherwise, or suggest a particular course of action in any specific situation, nor is this book meant as a substitute for any professional advice, medical or otherwise. The reader accepts all responsibility for how he or she chooses to use the information contained in this book and under no circumstances will the author or publisher be held liable for any damages caused directly or indirectly by any information contained in this book.

30 Day Whole Food Challenge

Sign up to get healthy living tips and tricks as well as a free bonus ebook at:

www.albertpino.com

30 Day Whole Food Challenge

Table of Contents

What is a whole food diet?...........16

Grains..16
Legumes...17
Fruits and Vegetables......................17
Nuts and Seeds...............................18
Nutrient requirements vs caloric requirements.........18
Exercise and Activity.......................19

Benefits of a Whole Food Diet...........22

Why is vitamin B12 important?........................22
What about oils?............................23
That "whole food high".................23

The 30 day whole food challenge...........26

Day 1...........28

Breakfast: Berry Smoothie and Cinnamon Toast..........28
Lunch: Shredded Yellow Curry Chicken Salad..........29
Dinner: Fresh Snapper Ceviche........................30
Juice: Citrus Peppermint.................32

Day 2...........34

Breakfast: Spinach Omelet and Avocado..........34
Lunch: Smashed Garlic Pinto Bean Pita..........35
Dinner: Mediterranean Quinoa Pitas 36
Juice: Kale Mint..........................38

Day 3...........40

Breakfast: Berry Baked Custard..........40

Lunch: Lively Pumpkin Seed Salad..42
Dinner: Rawlicious Spinach Stuffed Portobello Caps............43
Juice: Kale Cocktail..45

Day 4..46

Breakfast: Almond Raisin Oatmeal..46
Lunch: Perfect Pesto Pasta..47
Dinner: Super Simple Chickpea Salad Pitas..........................49
Juice: Pomegranate Cheer...50

Day 5..52

Breakfast: Baked Apple Pancakes...52
Lunch: Kale Wrapped Navy Beans..54
Dinner: Lemon Pepper Kale and Garlic Salmon....................56
Juice: Green and Beets..58

Day 6..60

Breakfast: Tasty and Healthy Whole Wheat Breakfast Crepes
....60
Lunch: Red Lentil Soup..62
Dinner: Toasty Kale Pecan Squash...63
Juice: Cranberry Parsnip...65

Day 7..66

Breakfast: Raspberry Chia Seed Pudding...............................66
Lunch: Delicious Cauliflower and Celery Fat Loss Soup.......67
Dinner: South of the Border Spicy Pinto Beans.....................69
Juice: Rock the Cabbage...70

Day 8..72

Breakfast: Creamy Cashew Parfait...72
Lunch: Quinoa Protein Power Patty...73
Dinner: Vegan Tofu Tacos..75
Juice: Manganese Mania..77

Day 9...78

Breakfast: Oat Cranberry Smoothie.......................78
Lunch: Healthy High Fiber Hummus.......................79
Dinner: Vegan Chickpea Salad................................80
Juice: Down to Earth...81

Day 10...82

Breakfast: Banana Quinoa.....................................82
Lunch: Sweet Potato Powerhouse Mash................83
Dinner: Cracked Pepper Quinoa Salmon Cakes....84
Juice: Coconut Lifestyle..86

Day 11...88

Breakfast: Almond Raisin Oatmeal.......................88
Lunch: Smashed Garlic Pinto Bean Pita................89
Dinner: Lemon Pepper Kale and Garlic Salmon....90
Juice: Green, Rested, and Ready...........................92

Day 12...94

Breakfast: Baked Apple Pancakes.........................94
Lunch: Shredded Yellow Curry Chicken Salad......96
Dinner: Super Simple Chickpea Salad Pitas..........97
Juice: The Fennel Cleanse.....................................98

Day 13...100

Breakfast: Tasty and Healthy Whole Wheat Breakfast Crepes
....100
Lunch: Lively Pumpkin Seed Salad......................102
Dinner: Mediterranean Quinoa Pitas 103
Juice: Emerald City..105

Day 14...106

Breakfast: Raspberry Chia Seed Pudding............106

Lunch: Kale Wrapped Navy Beans.....................................107
Dinner: Rawlicious Spinach Stuffed Portobello Caps...........109
Juice: Jumping Vegetable Juice......................................111

Day 15...112

Breakfast: Berry Smoothie and Cinnamon Toast.................112
Lunch: Perfect Pesto Pasta..113
Dinner: Fresh Snapper Ceviche......................................115
Juice: Taiwanese Treat..117

Day 16...118

Breakfast: Spinach Omelet and Avocado...........................118
Lunch: Healthy High Fiber Hummus.................................119
Dinner: Cracked Pepper Quinoa Salmon Cakes...................120
Juice: Cruciferous Kale Juice...122

Day 17...124

Breakfast: Berry Baked Custard......................................124
Lunch: Sweet Potato Powerhouse Mash.............................126
Dinner: Vegan Chickpea Salad..127
Juice: Cruciferous Cabbage Juice....................................128

Day 18...130

Breakfast: Tasty and Healthy Whole Wheat Breakfast Crepes
....130
Lunch: Red Lentil Soup...132
Dinner: South of the Border Spicy Pinto Beans...................133
Juice: Sargent Peppermint...134

Day 19...136

Breakfast: Raspberry Chia Seed Pudding...........................136
Lunch: Delicious Cauliflower and Celery Fat Loss Soup.....137
Dinner: Vegan Tofu Tacos..139
Juice: Sourpuss Supreme...141

Day 20 142

Breakfast: Creamy Cashew Parfait 142
Lunch: Quinoa Protein Power Patty 143
Dinner: Toasty Kale Pecan Squash 145
Juice: Simple Farmer 147

Day 21 148

Breakfast: Oat Cranberry Smoothie 148
Lunch: Lively Pumpkin Seed Salad 149
Dinner: Lemon Pepper Kale and Garlic Salmon 150
Juice: Superhero's Secret 152

Day 22 154

Breakfast: Banana Quinoa 154
Lunch: Smashed Garlic Pinto Bean Pita 155
Dinner: Fresh Snapper Ceviche 156
Juice: ABC Juice (Asparagus, Broccoli, Cucumber) 158

Day 23 160

Breakfast: Almond Raisin Oatmeal 160
Lunch: Shredded Yellow Curry Chicken Salad 161
Dinner: Super Simple Chickpea Salad Pitas 162
Juice: Pink Hijinx 163

Day 24 164

Breakfast: Baked Apple Pancakes 164
Lunch: Red Lentil Soup 166
Dinner: Rawlicious Spinach Stuffed Portobello Caps 167
Juice: Cruciferous Craze 169

Day 25 170

Breakfast: Tasty and Healthy Whole Wheat Breakfast Crepes
.... 170

Lunch: Kale Wrapped Navy Beans......................................172
Dinner: Mediterranean Quinoa Pitas 174
Juice: Spinach Ginger Zing-a-linger...............................176

Day 26...178
Breakfast: Spinach Omelet and Avocado............................178
Lunch: Perfect Pesto Pasta...179
Dinner: South of the Border Spicy Pinto Beans.................181
Juice: Pepper and Cabbage...182

Day 27...184
Breakfast: Raspberry Chia Seed Pudding..........................184
Lunch: Sweet Potato Powerhouse Mash............................185
Dinner: Cracked Pepper Quinoa Salmon Cakes..................186
Juice: Mister Cruciferous...188

Day 28...190
Breakfast: Oat Cranberry Smoothie..................................190
Lunch: Healthy High Fiber Hummus.................................191
Dinner: Vegan Chickpea Salad...192
Juice: Mighty Toxin Slayer...193

Day 29...194
Breakfast: Banana Quinoa...194
Lunch: Quinoa Protein Power Patty..................................195
Dinner: Toasty Kale Pecan Squash....................................197
Juice: The Scale Loves Kale...199

Day 30...200
Breakfast: Almond Raisin Oatmeal...................................200
Lunch: Healthy High Fiber Hummus.................................201
Dinner: Vegan Tofu Tacos...202
Juice: Sprout Celebration...204

Conclusion...206
One Final Thing...208

30 Day Whole Food Challenge

What is a whole food diet?

Let's make this as simple as possible. Because we so routinely break food into macro-nutrient categories (that is to say, fats, carbohydrates, and protein) people often get confused about how to eat. Let's take a moment to put things back together so that we can dispense with the understanding of food as a macro-nutrient category, and appreciate the food for what it really is – food!

Whole foods are unprocessed foods that come from the earth. There are some minimally processed foods that we are going to include in our whole food diet. These include breads, pastas, non-diary milk, non-diary butter, and tofu.

All of these categories are what makes up a whole food diet. The fun part (and also the challenging part for many) is how we combine, prepare, and cook these foods in order to create meals that are not just healthy but also delicious, filling, and with enough variety that you don't get bored and start getting tempted by unhealthy, highly processed junk foods.

Grains

I'm going to touch on these categories briefly. Let's start with the grains. This category includes foods like:
- oats
- brown rice
- quinoa
- whole wheat pasta
- whole grain breads
- pita

I should point out that quinoa is technically a seed. I like to think of it as a grain though, as I find it is typically consumed as if it were a grain. For that reason, we'll include it in the grain category.

Legumes

The second category I'll deal with here is legumes. This category includes foods like:
- beans
- lentils
- tofu

It is worth noting that both of the above categories – grains and legumes – have attracted some amount of controversy among devotees to a whole food diet. I have to say that any counsel to avoid whole grains and legumes is simply poor advice and not backed up by the weight of nutritional science. Foods like beans, lentils, and quinoa earn top marks for being nutrient-dense while very low in calories. These are supremely healthy foods and I encourage you to enjoy them without any guilt!

Fruits and Vegetables

The third category is the classic category of food associated with healthy eating: fruits and vegetables. We all have a pretty good idea about what fruits and vegetables are for the most part, but did you know that in addition to the usual suspects, this category also includes:
- dates
- bok choy

- pomegranate
- guava

Nuts and Seeds

The fourth category is nuts and seeds. Nuts are an excellent source of natural, healthy fat and tend to be overlooked when we think about healthy eating. They shouldn't be! Nuts have been shown to promote weight loss, heart health, and improved cholesterol levels. There are a wide variety of nuts and seeds that are great for your health, but raw tree nuts tend to be among the healthiest. Raw tree nuts include nuts like:

- cashews
- walnuts
- almonds

Nutrient requirements vs caloric requirements

Your daily nutrient requirement is the nutrients your body needs on a daily basis in order to sustain the body's health. It is important to realize that this is something totally separate from caloric requirement. The caloric requirement is simply the number of calories your body must ingest in order to avoid triggering an unhealthy starvation mode. As both of these requirements are separate, it is possible to achieve either one and not the other, or to achieve neither, or both.

A person who has achieved their daily nutrient requirement but not their daily caloric requirement has likely done so by eating many nutrient-dense foods. Nutrient-dense foods are foods that contain many nutrients and not many calories. Examples of particularly nutrient-dense foods includes kale, cabbage, broccoli, romaine lettuce, and cauliflower.

A person who has achieved their daily caloric requirement but not their daily nutrient requirement has likely done so by eating many calorie-dense foods. Calorie-dense foods are foods that contain many calories, but not many nutrients. These foods are often thought of as "junk food" and are often highly processed. Examples include potato chips, sugar, fast foods, etc. Even some whole foods can be thought of as calorie-dense however, such as potatoes, oats, beans, lentils, breads, and pasta.

A good strategy to ensure you get the nutrients your body requires is to focus on filling up your daily nutrient requirement before you fill up your daily caloric requirement. That means make sure you are eating a good amount of nutrient-dense food before you start eating more calorie-dense food. This can be done by structuring meals such that you consume nutrient-dense foods earlier in the day, or it can be done by simply eating the nutrient-dense foods before the more calorie-dense foods when the two are part of the same meal. This option makes more sense if you know you are going to be engaging in strenuous activity during the day and you don't want to put off consuming the calorie-dense foods your body will need as fuel.

Exercise and Activity

If you exercise a lot, your body will require greater caloric intake than someone who is more sedentary. This means it is even more important for you to consume healthy foods in order to prevent consuming a caloric surplus of unhealthy foods. By focusing on eating healthy whole foods and eating your nutrient-dense foods first, you can stop worrying about counting calories and rest assured that not only are you getting the nutrients your body needs, but that you are also not putting yourself in jeopardy of weight gain or the many health consequences that come from eating poorly.

30 Day Whole Food Challenge

Benefits of a Whole Food Diet

When you eat a whole food diet, as you'll learn to do in this book, you will experience a wide array of health and lifestyle advantages. When your kitchen is stocked with clean, healthy, whole foods, all you really need to worry about is how to prepare it. You'll be free of dealing with food addictions like addictions to sugar and salt. It is an interesting fact about the Standard American Diet that when you consume highly processed food the body doesn't know when to stop eating. The high levels of chemicals, salt, and sugar tricks our body into thinking it still needs to eat when in fact the body as already received more than enough calories.

When you eat whole foods on a regular basis, you can forget all about carbs, proteins, fat, and calorie counting forever! Furthermore, the only supplements you may need to keep in mind on a whole food diet is vitamin B12 and vitamin D. If you are vegetarian, vegan, or you just don't eat much meat you may want to take a vitamin B12 supplement. If you live in a cold climate, or you don't get much sunshine, you may want to take a vitamin D supplement.

Why is vitamin B12 important?

B12 comes from microbes that are found in various natural places like earth and river water. The unfortunate thing about modern society is that we have become far removed from natural sources of nutrients like B12. We don't drink from rivers and we generally don't consume organic fruits and vegetables fresh from the ground. For these reasons it can be helpful to supplement for B12, especially if you don't eat much meat. It is always a good idea to get your blood levels checked before beginning any supplementation regime.

What about oils?

Oils can be used sparingly as part of a whole food, primarily plant based diet. Some argue that oils are not whole foods. In fact in most cases this is clearly correct and many oils should be avoided for this reason. Most oils are highly processed and sold commercially in a heavily concentrated form.

There is some amount of controversy surrounding advice relating to oil, whether the advice is to consume it or abstain from it. Many nutritionists agree however that certain oils do have health benefits with few (if any) drawbacks. Ultimately, whether you want to use oil or not is a personal choice. If you otherwise eat a healthy whole food diet, including oil or not is unlikely to impact significantly on your health either way as long as you follow a few simple guidelines. The only important advice I would strongly suggest you follow when it comes to oil is that if you do choose to use oil, use as little as possible and also use only minimally processed oils, such as extra virgin olive oil. Completely avoid highly processed oils like vegetable oil.

That "whole food high"

The feeling of living life on a whole food diet is incredible. In fact, many people describe it as an energy "high" that they have never felt before. Simply put, eating whole foods feels amazing! After a few weeks, or even a few days, you can expect to feel dramatically more energetic. A feeling of mental clarity and endurance will follow and you will notice your ability to sustain longer sessions of peak intellectual and creative output.

In the long term, you can expect to get fewer colds and flus and to recover from injuries and illness faster than before. You can also expect your longevity to increase. You will live a longer life and a higher quality of life on the whole food diet than virtually any other diet or lifestyle. Not only that, the whole food diet is sustainable indefinitely because there is no starvation calorie restriction, no bizarre demands based on eating certain foods at certain times of day, and no slavish avoidance of entire macro-nutrient categories. Once you know how to prepare enough healthy and delicious whole food meals to go for a month without getting bored, you'll have all you need to know to stick with the whole food diet long term and start living a longer, higher quality life – I guarantee it!

30 Day Whole Food Challenge

The 30 day whole food challenge

I'm calling it a challenge, but really there isn't much of a challenge to eating this way. The recipes are not that hard to learn as they do not require any elaborate preparation or exotic ingredients or equipment. The dishes you'll make will be delicious, not at all plain or boring. Most importantly, they will make you feel great.

What follows in this book is a complete plan for living a whole food lifestyle for 30 days. Each day contains a recipe for a tasty and nutritious breakfast, lunch, and dinner. Each day also contains a recipe for a fresh juice you can whip up in your juicer and consume either with a meal or by itself as a snack between meals. Juicing is a great way to ensure you never miss out on your daily nutrient requirement regardless of how much or little you eat at meal times. For each of the juicing recipes, simply wash the fresh fruit and vegetables you're using and insert all of the ingredients in your juicer. If you don't own a juicer, you could skip the juices and still enjoy many health and weight loss benefits that come with the whole food diet. I'd encourage you to pick up a juicer and get serious about juicing though. Centrifugal juicers can be bought at retail for less than $100, cheaper if you can find one second hand.

If you're curious to learn more about juicing or want access to almost two years worth of recipes for the price of a latte, check out one of my other books I co-wrote with "Fat Loss" Frankie, who went from morbidly obese to trim and fit by doing a juice cleanse using many of the recipes in the book. The book is called *Juice Up! 500 Juicing Recipes* and it is available now on Amazon.

With all of the basics out of the way, you're now ready to begin your 30 day whole food challenge. Good luck and enjoy! I'll see you on the other side!

Day 1

Breakfast: Berry Smoothie and Cinnamon Toast

INGREDIENTS

1.5 cups plain organic yogurt

1 cup berries, fresh or frozen (blueberries, raspberries, or any other berry you life)

2 bananas

2 tablespoons milk

0.5 to 0.75 cup fresh spinach leaves

INSTRUCTIONS

Combine all ingredients into blender and blend until smooth. Drink with a piece of cinnamon raisin toast, or other whole grain toast with cinnamon sprinkled on it. You could also spread a nut butter on the toast if you want some additional flavor.

Lunch: Shredded Yellow Curry Chicken Salad

INGREDIENTS

3 cups chicken, cooked and shredded

0.25 cups plain yogurt

1 teaspoon yellow curry powder

Handful of cilantro leaves, thoroughly washed

Handful of sliced almonds

INSTRUCTIONS

Simply combine the ingredients and toss for a delicious salad. If you'd like to add dressing, you can make your own simple, tasty, healthy dressing by combining 1 tablespoon of extra virgin olive oil mixed with 2 teaspoons of balsamic vinegar.

Dinner: Fresh Snapper Ceviche

INGREDIENTS

Approximately 750g of fresh snapper, ensure all bones are removed and cut the meat into small cubes between 1 and 1.5 cm each

Juice from three fresh, medium sized limes

1.5 cups of coconut water

2 tablespoons of coriander leaves, chopped

2 tablespoons of mint leaves, chopped

4 spring onions, sliced fine

1 small red chili, sliced fine

Pinch of ground course sea salt

SALSA INGREDIENTS (if using as a dip)

1 ripe avocado, dice the flesh of the avocado into cubes of 1-2 cm each

1 red capsicum, diced

2 tablespoons chopped coriander

Juice from half a lime (lime zest to taste)

INSTRUCTIONS

Mix herbs, chili, lime juice, coconut water, and spring onions, in small bowl.

Add fish to mix and ensure all cubes are thoroughly coated.

Cover and refrigerate for 3-5 hours.

Garnish with additional coriander and mint to taste. Serve on it's own or as a dip with your favorite vegetables, or shrimp if you want additional protein.

Juice: Citrus Peppermint

One large pink grapefruit
One clementine (or substitute for a small orange, or half a large orange)
Six leaves of peppermint
Two cloves of garlic

30 Day Whole Food Challenge

Day 2

Breakfast: Spinach Omelet and Avocado

INGREDIENTS

2 eggs (best if you can purchase them from a local farmer's market)

2 Avocados

Handful of organic spinach

Big pinch of parsley

INSTRUCTIONS

Mix the yolks and egg whites in a bowl (or discard the yolks if you prefer). Pour eggs into a frying pan, top with spinach leaves and parsley. Slice both avocados in half and serve.

Lunch: Smashed Garlic Pinto Bean Pita

INGREDIENTS

1 onion, chopped

2 cups dry pinto beans (make sure you rinse them well and check for rocks)

Handful of fresh jalapeno peppers, chopped

4 cloves garlic, smashed and minced

1 teaspoon black pepper

1 teaspoon chili pepper

Two tablespoons of cumin

6 cups of water or your favorite broth

INSTRUCTIONS

Combine all ingredients in slow cooker and cook on high for at least 6 hours (8 hours is best).

Drain any excess liquid. Serve in a bowl or in a warm, whole wheat pita.

Dinner: Mediterranean Quinoa Pitas

INGREDIENTS

0.5 cup quinoa, washed

1 medium sized chopped carrot

5 scallions, sliced thin

2 cups of any white beans (i.e. navy beans), as always ensure your beans are thoroughly washed and inspected for rocks

0.25 cups of whole grain bread crumbs

1 egg, preferably from your local farmers market

2 tablespoons extra virgin olive oil

Half an English cucumber, cut in diagonal thin slices

Ground coarse sea salt to taste

Dash of ground pepper, to taste

1 tablespoon ground cumin

0.5 cup of plain Greek yogurt

1 tablespoon fresh lemon juice

4 whole wheat pitas

INSTRUCTIONS

Cook quinoa according to instructions on package, then set aside.

Process carrot in your food processor until pieces are finely chopped, then add the cooked quinoa, egg, beans, breadcrumbs, cumin, 1 teaspoon of ground sea salt, a quarter of a teaspoon of pepper and half the scallions. Process until the ingredients are mixed, but still chunky.

Spoon the mixture into four patties, then refrigerate for 15 minutes to firm them up if necessary.

Heat oil in a pan over medium heat, then brown the patties, 6-8 minutes per side.

Mix lemon juice, Greek yogurt, and the other half of the scallions; season with ground coarse sea salt and pepper to taste.

Portion the mixture into the pitas, add one of the patties to each pita and serve.

Juice: Kale Mint

Eight leaves of kale
One cup of fresh mint leaves
One cup of broccoli florets
One English cucumber
One medium sized green bell pepper
Two cups of spinach
One lemon, peeled

30 Day Whole Food Challenge

Day 3

Breakfast: Berry Baked Custard

INGREDIENTS

4 eggs (preferably from a local farmer's market)

1 cup of Greek yogurt

0.5 teaspoons of vanilla powder

Finely grated zest of one lemon

30 blueberries, fresh or frozen (thawed overnight in the fridge)

INSTRUCTIONS (makes four servings)

Preheat your oven to 200°C.

In a food processor or blender, mix the eggs, yogurt, vanilla and lemon zest for 45 seconds

Grease the ramekins with a small amount of almond butter

Pour the mixture into four ramekins. Place the ramekins in a large ovenproof pan with lid, filled with water such that the water level reaches the top quarter of the ramekins

Place some fruit in each ramekin

Cover with the lid and bake for about 30 minutes or until the middle is set and beginning to rise

Lunch: Lively Pumpkin Seed Salad

INGREDIENTS

3 cups of your favorite lettuce leaves, mixed greens, or spinach
0.25 cups roasted pumpkin seeds
0.25 cups currants

Dressing: 1 tablespoon extra virgin olive oil mixed with 2 teaspoons balsamic vinegar

INSTRUCTIONS

Simply chop the lettuce, mix all ingredients and serve!

Dinner: Rawlicious Spinach Stuffed Portobello Caps

INGREDIENTS

4 portobello mushroom caps

Juice three fresh medium sized lemons and zest one teaspoon (or to taste)

Half a cup of cashews

5 tablespoons of extra virgin olive oil

3 mined cloves of garlic

2 sliced scallions

Pinch of ground course sea salt (or to taste)

2 teaspoons of fresh rosemary, chopped

1 cup of spinach leaves

1 cup of corn kernels

INSTRUCTIONS

Combine and whisk oil, rosemary, garlic, salt, lemon juice and zest.

Place the mushroom caps, rounded side facing down, in a baking

dish. Gently pierce each cap several times with a fork or the tip of a knife.

Pour the mixture in equal portions in the mushroom caps, then cover and refrigerate between 3 and 8 hours.

Soak cashews in warm water for 20-40 minutes. Drain the water and process in your food processor with 0.25 cups of fresh water until you have a smooth puree. Add some ground course sea salt to taste.

Spoon the cashew puree into the mushroom caps. Garnish the mushroom caps with spinach, corn, scallions, and serve.

Juice: Kale Cocktail

Seven leaves of kale
One cup of cranberries
One cup of spinach
Three large stalks of celery
One English cucumber
One lemon, peeled

Day 4

Breakfast: Almond Raisin Oatmeal

INGREDIENTS

Steel cut oatmeal

Handful of raisins

Handful of almonds

Cinnamon

INSTRUCTIONS

Prepare the oatmeal according to the instructions on the package. When the oatmeal is halfway finished cooking, add the raisins and almonds. When finished cooking, add cinnamon to taste

Lunch: Perfect Pesto Pasta

INGREDIENTS

Two cups of fresh sweet peas, cooked

1/2 cup extra virgin olive oil

1 handful of fresh basil

3 cloves of garlic, minced

Quarter cup pine nuts

Half teaspoon tsp onion powder

Half teaspoon garlic powder

Quarter cup red onion, finely diced

Handful of fresh cherry tomatoes

Pinch of sea salt

Your favorite pasta

INSTRUCTIONS

Mix the cooked sweet peas, basil, pine nuts, olive oil, garlic, onion powder and garlic powder in your blender.

Heat one tablespoon of extra virgin olive oil in a pan over

medium heat. Add diced onion to the pan.

After cooking for five minutes, add the cooked onion to the blender and blend.

Cook your pasta, then simply add your pesto from the blender to the cooked pasta, garnish with cherry tomatoes, toss thoroughly, and serve.

Dinner: Super Simple Chickpea Salad Pitas

INGREDIENTS

0.5 cups of chopped celery

1.5 cups of cooked chickpeas

1 medium sized dill pickle, chopped

1 garlic clove, minced

3 tablespoons of chopped red onion

1 tablespoon of fresh dill, minced

2 tablespoons of fresh lemon juice

0.5 cups of toasted sunflower seeds

Course ground sea salt and pepper to taste

INSTRUCTIONS

Preheat toaster oven to 325F/160C and toast your sunflower seeds for 8-10 minutes.

Mix all of the ingredients into a bowl

Spoon the mixture into some fresh whole wheat pitas and enjoy!

Juice: Pomegranate Cheer

One large pomegranate
One Red Delicious apple
Two large stalks of celery
One half of a lemon, peeled
Thumb sized piece of ginger root

30 Day Whole Food Challenge

Day 5

Breakfast: Baked Apple Pancakes

INGREDIENTS

2 Granny Smith apples, peeled and sliced paper thin

Approximately 4 tablespoons of almond butter, enough to cover your pan

3 eggs (preferably from a local farmer's market)

1 cup of coconut milk

2 teaspoons of cinnamon

3 tablespoons of coconut sugar (according to taste)

1 teaspoon of juice from freshly squeezed lemon

1 teaspoon of vanilla powder

half a teaspoon of sea salt

half a teaspoon of bicarbonate of soda

2 cups of almond meal

INSTRUCTIONS

Preheat oven to 180°C.

In an oven-proof pan melt the almond butter. It should coat the base of the pan completely

Cover the base of the pan in a single layer of apple slices. Sprinkle cinnamon and coconut sugar over the apple slices

In a blender or food processor, combine the eggs, milk, almond meal, remaining sugar, cinnamon, vanilla, sea salt, bicarbonate of soda. vinegar and mix until thoroughly combined.

Pour the mix over the apple slices.

Bake in your preheated oven for approximately 20 minutes or until the middle of the pancake is set

Lunch: Kale Wrapped Navy Beans

INGREDIENTS

3 tbsp extra virgin olive oil

1 cup chopped onions

5 Cloves of garlic, minced

2-3 fresh whole tomatoes, blended

4 fresh basil leaves, chopped

Half teaspoon ground sage

2 cups cooked navy beans (cook for 6-8 hours in slow cooker)

INSTRUCTIONS

Add 3 tablespoons of olive oil and chopped onions to pot with lid and warm over low heat

Add garlic and saute until fragrant but not burnt.

Add tomatoes, sage, and basil leaves, stir and simmer for 5 minutes

Add cooked beans

Stir and simmer for 20 minutes

Spoon mix into leaves of kale, wrap and serve

Dinner: Lemon Pepper Kale and Garlic Salmon

INGREDIENTS

1 salmon fillet

Half a bunch of fresh kale, chopped

1 red bell pepper, sliced

5 cloves of garlic, finely chopped

Juice from one medium sized freshly squeezed lemon

1-2 tablespoons of almond butter

Half a red onion, diced

3 tablespoons of lemon pepper (or to taste)

INSTRUCTIONS

In a non-stick pan, or a pan lightly coated extra virgin olive oil, fry the salmon fillet 3-5 minutes per side over medium heat. With one minute left of cooking, add half the finely chopped garlic and lemon juice to the pan, then spoon over salmon fillet when serving.

Melt the almond butter in a pan over medium-low heat and add onion and red bell pepper.

After 3 minutes, add the chopped kale and the other half of the

garlic. Sprinkle with lemon pepper.

Use tongs to turn and mix the kale with the other ingredients in the pan. Ensure the kale is heated evenly. Remove after only 2 minutes.

Serve and enjoy! For more lemon flavor, garnish the salmon fillet with a thin slice of lemon and sprinkle with lemon pepper.

Juice: Green and Beets

Two beetroot
Three leaves of kale
Four leaves of Romaine lettuce
One English cucumber
Two large stalks of celery
One cup of cranberries
Two large sized carrots

30 Day Whole Food Challenge

Day 6

Breakfast: Tasty and Healthy Whole Wheat Breakfast Crepes

INGREDIENTS

3 eggs (preferably from a local farmer's market)

1 cup whole-wheat flour

1 cup almond milk

1 teaspoon vanilla

A quarter of a teaspoon of salt

Half a cup of water

2 tablespoons of melted almond butter

INSTRUCTIONS

Put all of the ingredients in your blender and mix them thoroughly. Let the mix stand for 10 minutes.
Coat your frying pan with almond butter over medium heat.

Pour the batter on your pan held at an angle. Swirl the batter around to coat the entire the pan in one thin layer.

Push down the thin edges of the crepe around the perimeter using

a spatula.

After 45 seconds to 1 minute when the crepe is golden brown on the bottom, flip it over. Do this delicately to avoid ripping the crepe.

Cook another 45 seconds on the other side and then roll up each crepe.

Lunch: Red Lentil Soup

INGREDIENTS

1 cup red lentils, washed thoroughly

3 celery stalks, chopped

1 large onion, chopped

2 large carrots, chopped

2 tablespoons of tomato paste

2 cups of broccoli florets

Pinch of oregano

1 bay leaf

6 leaves of basil, chopped

Pinch of ground thyme

5 cups water

INSTRUCTIONS

Simply combine ingredients in a slow cooker and cook for 4-5 hours on high. Enjoy!

Dinner: Toasty Kale Pecan Squash

INGREDIENTS

1 medium sized butternut squash

3 garlic cloves, minced

4 tablespoons fresh parsley, chopped

Pinch of ground course sea salt (or to taste)

Half a tablespoon of extra virgin olive oil

1 cup of fresh chopped kale

ADDITIONAL INGREDIENTS TO BE PROCESSED:

1 tablespoon of nutritional yeast

0.25 cups of almonds

0.25 cups of pecans

1 teaspoon of extra virgin olive oil

Pinch of ground course sea salt

INSTRUCTIONS

Preheat oven to 400F/205C and lightly coat your casserole dish

with oil

Peel the squash, remove the top and bottom, then cut into two halves. Scoop out the guts and seeds. Further chop the two halves of squash into cubes of about 3 cm each and add the cubes to the casserole dish.

Add parsley, salt, minced garlic, and oil into the casserole dish and stir until well mixed with the squash cubes.

Cover and bake for 40-50 minutes.

While baking, combine the pecans, almonds, yeast, as well as a pinch of salt and 1 teaspoon of extra virgin olive oil in your food processor until chunky. Do not puree.

After 40-50 minutes, remove squash from the oven and turn off the heat. Add the chopped kale and sprinkle the mixture from the food processor all over the squash. Then return to the still hot oven for 10 5 minutes to warm the processed ingredients.

Serve and enjoy!

Juice: Cranberry Parsnip

Two parsnips
One cup of cranberries
Four medium sized carrots
Four large stalks of celery
One lemon, peeled

Day 7

Breakfast: Raspberry Chia Seed Pudding

INGREDIENTS

1.5 cups fresh or frozen raspberries (if frozen, thaw overnight in the fridge)

1.5 cups of coconut milk

0.5 cups of chia seeds

1 teaspoon of vanilla powder

0.25 cups of brown rice syrup (according to taste)

INSTRUCTIONS

Mix all ingredients thoroughly in a blender

Refrigerate overnight to allow the mix to thicken

Consume in the morning for a fast, simple, delicious, and healthy breakfast!

Lunch: Delicious Cauliflower and Celery Fat Loss Soup

INGREDIENTS

1 large cauliflower (between 2 and 3 pounds)

3 medium onions, chopped

3 celery stalks, chopped

1 teaspoon of paprika

1 teaspoon of onion powder

1 teaspoon of garlic powder

2 tablespoons of coconut oil

1 tablespoon of white wine vinegar

4 cups of water

1 bay leaf

2 garlic cloves, minced

1 tablespoon of freshly squeezed lime juice

Ground course sea salt according to taste

INSTRUCTIONS

Heat a medium sized dutch oven and pour in the coconut oil, then add onions and celery and cook for 3 minutes, then add garlic and cook for an additional one minute

Add the vinegar and stir until it evaporates

Stir in all the spices

Add the chopped cauliflower, salt, bay leaf, and water. Heat until it boils

Lower heat, cover, and simmer.

When the cauliflower is soft, remove bay leaf and stir to make the soup's texture more creamy, then serve

Dinner: South of the Border Spicy Pinto Beans

INGREDIENTS

1 pound pinto beans, washed and inspected for rocks

2 cups of fresh diced tomatoes

6 diced green chili peppers

1 large chopped yellow onion

1 1/2 teaspoons garlic powder

1 tablespoon ground cumin

1 tablespoon chili powder

INSTRUCTIONS

Soak beans overnight in a bowl of water, fully immersed

Place the drained beans in your crock pot, add fresh water such that all the beans are immersed, then add the onion, tomatoes, cumin, chili powder, and garlic powder.

Cook on high for 7-8 hours

Serve alone or in a whole wheat pita

Juice: Rock the Cabbage

Four large leaves of red cabbage
One beetroot
Three large stalk of celery
Half an English cucumber
One medium carrot
One large orange
One quarter of a pineapple
Two handfuls of spinach
Half a lemon, peeled

30 Day Whole Food Challenge

Day 8

Breakfast: Creamy Cashew Parfait

INGREDIENTS

1 cup of muesli

1 cup of cashew nut cream

1 cup of mixed frozen berries (do not thaw)

Quarter of a cup of toasted almond flakes

Ground cinnamon (to taste)

INSTRUCTIONS

Simply combine the ingredients, stir, and serve!

Lunch: Quinoa Protein Power Patty

INGREDIENTS

1 cup quinoa, (make sure you wash thoroughly first!)

1 bunch of spring onions (dice the white portion)

1 cup of chopped kale

4 eggs, preferably from your local farmer's market

2 cloves of garlic, chopped

1 cup of your favorite fresh whole grain bread crumbs

Ground course sea salt, to taste

Ground pepper, to taste

INSTRUCTIONS

Cook your washed quinoa according to the instructions on the package. After it is cooked, let it cool.

Stir your eggs in a bowl.

Mix all the ingredients together, including eggs and quinoa, stirring thoroughly.

Heat a large frying pan over medium heat. Add some minimally processed oil such as coconut oil if you like.

73

Spoon a portion of the mixture into the pan, using a spatula to press it down into the shape of a patty.

Cook until the edges start to brown, then flip and cook the other side until the edges start to brown.

Serve alone or on a whole grain bun or pita

Dinner: Vegan Tofu Tacos

INGREDIENTS

1 cup of cooked black beans

8 ounces of firm tofu

Half a medium sized red onion, diced

1 cup fresh cilantro, chopped

1 or 2 sliced avocados

0.25 cup of pomegranate seeds

Half a cup of salsa

Corn tortillas

SEASONING FOR TOFU:

Half a teaspoon of chili powder

1 teaspoon of cumin

1 teaspoon of garlic powder

Pinch of ground course sea salt

1 tablespoon of salsa

1 tablespoon of water

INSTRUCTIONS

Wrap tofu in a clean, absorbent towel and place something heavy on top, such as a cast iron skillet, while prepping toppings.

Cook black beans according to instructions on package, add a pinch each of salt, chili powder, cumin, and garlic powder, then set aside

Add the tofu seasoning and salsa to a bowl and top with just enough water to make a sauce that can be poured, then set aside.

Heat a pan over medium heat and add 1-2 tablespoons of oil and chopped tofu. Cook for 5 minutes, stirring frequently, then add seasoning. Cook for another 8 minutes, still stirring frequently.

Warm the tortillas and fill them with all of the ingredients, then serve and enjoy!

Juice: Manganese Mania

Two beetroot
Five medium sized carrots
One English cucumber
Three leaves of kale
One cup of broccoli florets
Two cloves of garlic

Day 9

Breakfast: Oat Cranberry Smoothie

INGREDIENTS

1 quarter cup of cranberries (fresh or frozen)

2 tablespoons rolled oats

1 cup almond milk

Half a pear

Dash of cinnamon (to taste)

INSTRUCTIONS

Simply combine all of the ingredients in a blender and blend until smooth. Enjoy!

Lunch: Healthy High Fiber Hummus

INGREDIENTS

1.5 cups of chickpeas (washed)

4 tablespoons of hulled tahini

1 clove of garlic, diced

Juice from one medium sized lemon

1 teaspoon cumin powder

Half a teaspoon of cinnamon powder

2 tablespoons of water

2 tablespoons of extra virgin olive oil

One pinch of ground course sea salt, or to taste

Black pepper to taste

INSTRUCTIONS

Simply use a food processor to thoroughly process all of the
ingredients, then serve

Dinner: Vegan Chickpea Salad

INGREDIENTS

3 cups cooked chickpeas

Half a cup of chopped sun dried tomatoes

3 tablespoons fresh squeezed lemon juice

15 fresh basil leaves, chopped

1 tablespoon of apple cider vinegar

2 tablespoons of extra virgin olive oil

Pinch of fresh ground pepper, to taste

INSTRUCTIONS

Blanch your sun dried tomatoes by placing them in a small bowl and pouring boiling fresh water over them, and soaking them for 5 minutes.

Drain the bowl, then slice the sun dried tomatoes.

Combine all ingredients including the sun dried tomatoes, serve and enjoy!

Juice: Down to Earth

Two medium sized apples, any variety
Two beetroot
Four large carrots
One third of a medium sized pineapple
One thumb sized piece of garlic

Day 10

Breakfast: Banana Quinoa

INGREDIENTS

1 cup cooked quinoa
1 cup almond milk
Handful of raisins
Dash of cinnamon (to taste)

INSTRUCTIONS

Use a small pan or pot and bring quinoa, milk, raisins, and cinnamon to a gentle boil. Once boiling, reduce the heat and simmer. Stir the mix frequently for about five minutes. You'll know it is done when about half the milk has been absorbed. Garnish with fresh slices of banana and serve.

Lunch: Sweet Potato Powerhouse Mash

INGREDIENTS

1 sweet potato (wash but don't peel)

1 teaspoon of coconut oil

1 tablespoon of almond butter

Ground course sea salt and freshly ground black pepper, to taste

INSTRUCTIONS

Preheat oven to 200°C/400°F

Using a fork, puncture the sweet potato 4 to 5 times to prevent it from exploding.

Bake on a tray for approximately 30 minutes. It is done when you can easily slide a fork into and out of the sweet potato

Remove from oven (be careful it will be very hot!) then cut and scoop out the flesh into a bowl. Add the coconut oil and almond butter, season with the salt and pepper, mash, and serve.

Dinner: Cracked Pepper Quinoa Salmon Cakes

INGREDIENTS

2 cups of fresh salmon, cooked and chopped into cubes of 1-2cm each

1 egg, preferably from you local farmer's market

Half a cup of quinoa flakes (or substitute for any variety of fast cooking oats)

1 tablespoon low sodium soy sauce

2 cloves of garlic, minced

0.25 cups of fresh chopped parsley

2 teaspoons of freshly ground pepper, or to taste

1 tablespoon extra virgin coconut oil

2 green onions, thinly sliced

INSTRUCTIONS

Combine all ingredients other than the oil and mix in a bowl

Spoon the mixture into patties (makes 6-8 patties)

Pour the oil in a medium sized pan and heat over medium-low heat.

Cook the salmon patties until golden brown, approximately 4 minutes per side.

Serve alone or in a warmed whole wheat pita with chopped romaine lettuce.

Juice: Coconut Lifestyle

One cup of fresh chopped coconut
Two medium sized carrots
Two Granny Smith apples
One clove of garlic
One thumb sized ginger

30 Day Whole Food Challenge

Day 11

Breakfast: Almond Raisin Oatmeal

INGREDIENTS

Steel cut oatmeal

Handful of raisins

Handful of almonds

Cinnamon

INSTRUCTIONS

Prepare the oatmeal according to the instructions on the package. When the oatmeal is halfway finished cooking, add the raisins and almonds. When finished cooking, add cinnamon to taste

Lunch: Smashed Garlic Pinto Bean Pita

INGREDIENTS

1 onion, chopped

2 cups dry pinto beans (make sure you rinse them well and check for rocks)

Handful of fresh jalapeno peppers, chopped

4 cloves garlic, smashed and minced

1 teaspoon black pepper

1 teaspoon chili pepper

Two tablespoons of cumin

6 cups of water or your favorite broth

INSTRUCTIONS

Combine all ingredients in slow cooker and cook on high for at least 6 hours (8 hours is best).

Drain any excess liquid. Serve in a bowl or in a warm, whole wheat pita.

Dinner: Lemon Pepper Kale and Garlic Salmon

INGREDIENTS

1 salmon fillet

Half a bunch of fresh kale, chopped

1 red bell pepper, sliced

5 cloves of garlic, finely chopped

Juice from one medium sized freshly squeezed lemon

1-2 tablespoons of almond butter

Half a red onion, diced

3 tablespoons of lemon pepper (or to taste)

INSTRUCTIONS

In a non-stick pan, or a pan lightly coated extra virgin olive oil, fry the salmon fillet 3-5 minutes per side over medium heat. With one minute left of cooking, add half the finely chopped garlic and lemon juice to the pan, then spoon over salmon fillet when serving.

Melt the almond butter in a pan over medium-low heat and add onion and red bell pepper.

After 3 minutes, add the chopped kale and the other half of the

garlic. Sprinkle with lemon pepper.

Use tongs to turn and mix the kale with the other ingredients in the pan. Ensure the kale is heated evenly. Remove after only 2 minutes.

Serve and enjoy! For more lemon flavor, garnish the salmon fillet with a thin slice of lemon and sprinkle with lemon pepper.

Juice: Green, Rested, and Ready

One English cucumber
Two cups of spinach
Two handfuls of parsley
Two medium sized Granny Smith apples
Two leaves of kale
One stalk of celery
Three stalks of asparagus

30 Day Whole Food Challenge

Day 12

Breakfast: Baked Apple Pancakes

INGREDIENTS

2 Granny Smith apples, peeled and sliced paper thin

Approximately 4 tablespoons of almond butter, enough to cover your pan

3 eggs (preferably from a local farmer's market)

1 cup of coconut milk

2 teaspoons of cinnamon

3 tablespoons of coconut sugar (according to taste)

1 teaspoon of juice from freshly squeezed lemon

1 teaspoon of vanilla powder

half a teaspoon of sea salt

half a teaspoon of bicarbonate of soda

2 cups of almond meal

INSTRUCTIONS

Preheat oven to 180°C.

In an oven-proof pan melt the almond butter. It should coat the base of the pan completely

Cover the base of the pan in a single layer of apple slices. Sprinkle cinnamon and coconut sugar over the apple slices

In a blender or food processor, combine the eggs, milk, almond meal, remaining sugar, cinnamon, vanilla, sea salt, bicarbonate of soda. vinegar and mix until thoroughly combined.

Pour the mix over the apple slices.

Bake in your preheated oven for approximately 20 minutes or until the middle of the pancake is set

Lunch: Shredded Yellow Curry Chicken Salad

INGREDIENTS

3 cups chicken, cooked and shredded

0.25 cups plain yogurt

1 teaspoon yellow curry powder

Handful of cilantro leaves, thoroughly washed

Handful of sliced almonds

INSTRUCTIONS

Simply combine the ingredients and toss for a delicious salad. If you'd like to add dressing, you can make your own simple, tasty, healthy dressing by combining 1 tablespoon of extra virgin olive oil mixed with 2 teaspoons of balsamic vinegar.

Dinner: Super Simple Chickpea Salad Pitas

INGREDIENTS

0.5 cups of chopped celery

1.5 cups of cooked chickpeas

1 medium sized dill pickle, chopped

1 garlic clove, minced

3 tablespoons of chopped red onion

1 tablespoon of fresh dill, minced

2 tablespoons of fresh lemon juice

0.5 cups of toasted sunflower seeds

Course ground sea salt and pepper to taste

INSTRUCTIONS

Preheat toaster oven to 325F/160C and toast your sunflower seeds for 8-10 minutes.

Mix all of the ingredients into a bowl

Spoon the mixture into some fresh whole wheat pitas and enjoy!

Juice: The Fennel Cleanse

One large cucumber
Three stalks of celery
Three medium sized Red Delicious apples
One fennel bulb and stem
One lime, peeled

30 Day Whole Food Challenge

Day 13

Breakfast: Tasty and Healthy Whole Wheat Breakfast Crepes

INGREDIENTS

3 eggs (preferably from a local farmer's market)

1 cup whole-wheat flour

1 cup almond milk

1 teaspoon vanilla

A quarter of a teaspoon of salt

Half a cup of water

2 tablespoons of melted almond butter

INSTRUCTIONS

Put all of the ingredients in your blender and mix them thoroughly. Let the mix stand for 10 minutes.
Coat your frying pan with almond butter over medium heat.

Pour the batter on your pan held at an angle. Swirl the batter around to coat the entire the pan in one thin layer.

Push down the thin edges of the crepe around the perimeter using

a spatula.

After 45 seconds to 1 minute when the crepe is golden brown on the bottom, flip it over. Do this delicately to avoid ripping the crepe.

Cook another 45 seconds on the other side and then roll up each crepe.

Lunch: Lively Pumpkin Seed Salad

INGREDIENTS

3 cups of your favorite lettuce leaves, mixed greens, or spinach
0.25 cups roasted pumpkin seeds
0.25 cups currants

Dressing: 1 tablespoon extra virgin olive oil mixed with 2 teaspoons balsamic vinegar

INSTRUCTIONS

Simply chop the lettuce, mix all ingredients and serve!

Dinner: Mediterranean Quinoa Pitas

INGREDIENTS

0.5 cup quinoa, washed

1 medium sized chopped carrot

5 scallions, sliced thin

2 cups of any white beans (i.e. navy beans), as always ensure your beans are thoroughly washed and inspected for rocks

0.25 cups of whole grain bread crumbs

1 egg, preferably from your local farmers market

2 tablespoons extra virgin olive oil

Half an English cucumber, cut in diagonal thin slices

Ground coarse sea salt to taste

Dash of ground pepper, to taste

1 tablespoon ground cumin

0.5 cup of plain Greek yogurt

1 tablespoon fresh lemon juice

4 whole wheat pitas

INSTRUCTIONS

Cook quinoa according to instructions on package, then set aside.

Process carrot in your food processor until pieces are finely chopped, then add the cooked quinoa, egg, beans, breadcrumbs, cumin, 1 teaspoon of ground sea salt, a quarter of a teaspoon of pepper and half the scallions. Process until the ingredients are mixed, but still chunky.

Spoon the mixture into four patties, then refrigerate for 15 minutes to firm them up if necessary.

Heat oil in a pan over medium heat, then brown the patties, 6-8 minutes per side.

Mix lemon juice, Greek yogurt, and the other half of the scallions; season with ground coarse sea salt and pepper to taste.

Portion the mixture into the pitas, add one of the patties to each pita and serve.

Juice: Emerald City

One English cucumber
Two cups of spinach
Two handfuls of parsley
Two medium sized Granny Smith apples
Two leaves of kale

Day 14

Breakfast: Raspberry Chia Seed Pudding

INGREDIENTS

1.5 cups fresh or frozen raspberries (if frozen, thaw overnight in the fridge)

1.5 cups of coconut milk

0.5 cups of chia seeds

1 teaspoon of vanilla powder

0.25 cups of brown rice syrup (according to taste)

INSTRUCTIONS

Mix all ingredients thoroughly in a blender

Refrigerate overnight to allow the mix to thicken

Consume in the morning for a fast, simple, delicious, and healthy breakfast!

Lunch: Kale Wrapped Navy Beans

INGREDIENTS

3 tbsp extra virgin olive oil

1 cup chopped onions

5 Cloves of garlic, minced

2-3 fresh whole tomatoes, blended

4 fresh basil leaves, chopped

Half teaspoon ground sage

2 cups cooked navy beans (cook for 6-8 hours in slow cooker)

INSTRUCTIONS

Add 3 tablespoons of olive oil and chopped onions to pot with lid and warm over low heat

Add garlic and saute until fragrant but not burnt.

Add tomatoes, sage, and basil leaves, stir and simmer for 5 minutes

Add cooked beans

Stir and simmer for 20 minutes

Spoon mix into leaves of kale, wrap and serve

Dinner: Rawlicious Spinach Stuffed Portobello Caps

INGREDIENTS

4 portobello mushroom caps

Juice three fresh medium sized lemons and zest one teaspoon (or to taste)

Half a cup of cashews

5 tablespoons of extra virgin olive oil

3 mined cloves of garlic

2 sliced scallions

Pinch of ground course sea salt (or to taste)

2 teaspoons of fresh rosemary, chopped

1 cup of spinach leaves

1 cup of corn kernels

INSTRUCTIONS

Combine and whisk oil, rosemary, garlic, salt, lemon juice and zest.

Place the mushroom caps, rounded side facing down, in a baking

dish. Gently pierce each cap several times with a fork or the tip of a knife.

Pour the mixture in equal portions in the mushroom caps, then cover and refrigerate between 3 and 8 hours.

Soak cashews in warm water for 20-40 minutes. Drain the water and process in your food processor with 0.25 cups of fresh water until you have a smooth puree. Add some ground course sea salt to taste.

Spoon the cashew puree into the mushroom caps. Garnish the mushroom caps with spinach, corn, scallions, and serve.

Juice: Jumping Vegetable Juice

One cup of spinach
Two salad tomatoes
One handful of parsley
One medium sized red bell pepper
Six large stalks of celery
Six stalks of asparagus
Half a cup of cranberries
Half a lemon, peeled

Day 15

Breakfast: Berry Smoothie and Cinnamon Toast

INGREDIENTS

1.5 cups plain organic yogurt

1 cup berries, fresh or frozen (blueberries, raspberries, or any other berry you life)

2 bananas

2 tablespoons milk

0.5 to 0.75 cup fresh spinach leaves

INSTRUCTIONS

Combine all ingredients into blender and blend until smooth. Drink with a piece of cinnamon raisin toast, or other whole grain toast with cinnamon sprinkled on it. You could also spread a nut butter on the toast if you want some additional flavor.

Lunch: Perfect Pesto Pasta

INGREDIENTS

Two cups of fresh sweet peas, cooked

1/2 cup extra virgin olive oil

1 handful of fresh basil

3 cloves of garlic, minced

Quarter cup pine nuts

Half teaspoon tsp onion powder

Half teaspoon garlic powder

Quarter cup red onion, finely diced

Handful of fresh cherry tomatoes

Pinch of sea salt

Your favorite pasta

INSTRUCTIONS

Mix the cooked sweet peas, basil, pine nuts, olive oil, garlic, onion powder and garlic powder in your blender.

Heat one tablespoon of extra virgin olive oil in a pan over

medium heat. Add diced onion to the pan.

After cooking for five minutes, add the cooked onion to the blender and blend.

Cook your pasta, then simply add your pesto from the blender to the cooked pasta, garnish with cherry tomatoes, toss thoroughly, and serve.

Dinner: Fresh Snapper Ceviche

INGREDIENTS

Approximately 750g of fresh snapper, ensure all bones are removed and cut the meat into small cubes between 1 and 1.5 cm each

Juice from three fresh, medium sized limes

1.5 cups of coconut water

2 tablespoons of coriander leaves, chopped

2 tablespoons of mint leaves, chopped

4 spring onions, sliced fine

1 small red chili, sliced fine

Pinch of ground course sea salt

SALSA INGREDIENTS (if using as a dip)

1 ripe avocado, dice the flesh of the avocado into cubes of 1-2 cm each

1 red capsicum, diced

2 tablespoons chopped coriander

Juice from half a lime (lime zest to taste)

INSTRUCTIONS

Mix herbs, chili, lime juice, coconut water, and spring onions, in small bowl.

Add fish to mix and ensure all cubes are thoroughly coated.

Cover and refrigerate for 3-5 hours.

Garnish with additional coriander and mint to taste. Serve on it's own or as a dip with your favorite vegetables, or shrimp if you want additional protein.

Juice: Taiwanese Treat

Three medium sized guava
One medium clementine, peeled
One medium sized apple, any variety
One lime, peeled

Day 16

Breakfast: Spinach Omelet and Avocado

INGREDIENTS

2 eggs (best if you can purchase them from a local farmer's market)

2 Avocados

Handful of organic spinach

Big pinch of parsley

INSTRUCTIONS

Mix the yolks and egg whites in a bowl (or discard the yolks if you prefer). Pour eggs into a frying pan, top with spinach leaves and parsley. Slice both avocados in half and serve.

Lunch: Healthy High Fiber Hummus

INGREDIENTS

1.5 cups of chickpeas (washed)

4 tablespoons of hulled tahini

1 clove of garlic, diced

Juice from one medium sized lemon

1 teaspoon cumin powder

Half a teaspoon of cinnamon powder

2 tablespoons of water

2 tablespoons of extra virgin olive oil

One pinch of ground course sea salt, or to taste

Black pepper to taste

INSTRUCTIONS

Simply use a food processor to thoroughly process all of the ingredients, then serve

Dinner: Cracked Pepper Quinoa Salmon Cakes

INGREDIENTS

2 cups of fresh salmon, cooked and chopped into cubes of 1-2cm each

1 egg, preferably from you local farmer's market

Half a cup of quinoa flakes (or substitute for any variety of fast cooking oats)

1 tablespoon low sodium soy sauce

2 cloves of garlic, minced

0.25 cups of fresh chopped parsley

2 teaspoons of freshly ground pepper, or to taste

1 tablespoon extra virgin coconut oil

2 green onions, thinly sliced

INSTRUCTIONS

Combine all ingredients other than the oil and mix in a bowl

Spoon the mixture into patties (makes 6-8 patties)

Pour the oil in a medium sized pan and heat over medium-low heat.

Cook the salmon patties until golden brown, approximately 4 minutes per side.

Serve alone or in a warmed whole wheat pita with chopped romaine lettuce.

Juice: Cruciferous Kale Juice

Eight leaves of kale
Fist-sized crown of broccoli
One English cucumber
One medium sized apples
One medium sized pear
Two cups of spinach
One lemon

30 Day Whole Food Challenge

Day 17

Breakfast: Berry Baked Custard

INGREDIENTS

4 eggs (preferably from a local farmer's market)

1 cup of Greek yogurt

0.5 teaspoons of vanilla powder

Finely grated zest of one lemon

30 blueberries, fresh or frozen (thawed overnight in the fridge)

INSTRUCTIONS (makes four servings)

Preheat your oven to 200°C.

In a food processor or blender, mix the eggs, yogurt, vanilla and lemon zest for 45 seconds

Grease the ramekins with a small amount of almond butter

Pour the mixture into four ramekins. Place the ramekins in a large ovenproof pan with lid, filled with water such that the water level reaches the top quarter of the ramekins

Place some fruit in each ramekin

Cover with the lid and bake for about 30 minutes or until the middle is set and beginning to rise

Lunch: Sweet Potato Powerhouse Mash

INGREDIENTS

1 sweet potato (wash but don't peel)

1 teaspoon of coconut oil

1 tablespoon of almond butter

Ground course sea salt and freshly ground black pepper, to taste

INSTRUCTIONS

Preheat oven to 200°C/400°F

Using a fork, puncture the sweet potato 4 to 5 times to prevent it from exploding.

Bake on a tray for approximately 30 minutes. It is done when you can easily slide a fork into and out of the sweet potato

Remove from oven (be careful it will be very hot!) then cut and scoop out the flesh into a bowl. Add the coconut oil and almond butter, season with the salt and pepper, mash, and serve.

Dinner: Vegan Chickpea Salad

INGREDIENTS

3 cups cooked chickpeas

Half a cup of chopped sun dried tomatoes

3 tablespoons fresh squeezed lemon juice

15 fresh basil leaves, chopped

1 tablespoon of apple cider vinegar

2 tablespoons of extra virgin olive oil

Pinch of fresh ground pepper, to taste

INSTRUCTIONS

Blanch your sun dried tomatoes by placing them in a small bowl and pouring boiling fresh water over them, and soaking them for 5 minutes.

Drain the bowl, then slice the sun dried tomatoes.

Combine all ingredients including the sun dried tomatoes, serve and enjoy!

Juice: Cruciferous Cabbage Juice

One quarter of a small head of green cabbage
Two medium sized Granny Smith apples
One cup of spinach
One thumb sized piece of ginger root
Two medium sized carrots
One stalk of celery
Half a lemon, peeled

30 Day Whole Food Challenge

Day 18

Breakfast: Tasty and Healthy Whole Wheat Breakfast Crepes

INGREDIENTS

3 eggs (preferably from a local farmer's market)

1 cup whole-wheat flour

1 cup almond milk

1 teaspoon vanilla

A quarter of a teaspoon of salt

Half a cup of water

2 tablespoons of melted almond butter

INSTRUCTIONS

Put all of the ingredients in your blender and mix them thoroughly. Let the mix stand for 10 minutes.
Coat your frying pan with almond butter over medium heat.

Pour the batter on your pan held at an angle. Swirl the batter around to coat the entire the pan in one thin layer.

Push down the thin edges of the crepe around the perimeter using

a spatula.

After 45 seconds to 1 minute when the crepe is golden brown on the bottom, flip it over. Do this delicately to avoid ripping the crepe.

Cook another 45 seconds on the other side and then roll up each crepe.

Lunch: Red Lentil Soup

INGREDIENTS

1 cup red lentils, washed thoroughly

3 celery stalks, chopped

1 large onion, chopped

2 large carrots, chopped

2 tablespoons of tomato paste

2 cups of broccoli florets

Pinch of oregano

1 bay leaf

6 leaves of basil, chopped

Pinch of ground thyme

5 cups water

INSTRUCTIONS

Simply combine ingredients in a slow cooker and cook for 4-5 hours on high. Enjoy!

Dinner: South of the Border Spicy Pinto Beans

INGREDIENTS

1 pound pinto beans, washed and inspected for rocks

2 cups of fresh diced tomatoes

6 diced green chili peppers

1 large chopped yellow onion

1 1/2 teaspoons garlic powder

1 tablespoon ground cumin

1 tablespoon chili powder

INSTRUCTIONS

Soak beans overnight in a bowl of water, fully immersed

Place the drained beans in your crock pot, add fresh water such that all the beans are immersed, then add the onion, tomatoes, cumin, chili powder, and garlic powder.

Cook on high for 7-8 hours

Serve alone or in a whole wheat pita

Juice: Sargent Peppermint

One medium sized orange
Five medium sized carrots
Three medium sized apples
Two large peaches
Half a lemon, peeled
One lime, peeled
Six leaves of peppermint

30 Day Whole Food Challenge

Day 19

Breakfast: Raspberry Chia Seed Pudding

INGREDIENTS

1.5 cups fresh or frozen raspberries (if frozen, thaw overnight in the fridge)

1.5 cups of coconut milk

0.5 cups of chia seeds

1 teaspoon of vanilla powder

0.25 cups of brown rice syrup (according to taste)

INSTRUCTIONS

Mix all ingredients thoroughly in a blender

Refrigerate overnight to allow the mix to thicken

Consume in the morning for a fast, simple, delicious, and healthy breakfast!

Lunch: Delicious Cauliflower and Celery Fat Loss Soup

INGREDIENTS

1 large cauliflower (between 2 and 3 pounds)

3 medium onions, chopped

3 celery stalks, chopped

1 teaspoon of paprika

1 teaspoon of onion powder

1 teaspoon of garlic powder

2 tablespoons of coconut oil

1 tablespoon of white wine vinegar

4 cups of water

1 bay leaf

2 garlic cloves, minced

1 tablespoon of freshly squeezed lime juice

Ground course sea salt according to taste

INSTRUCTIONS

Heat a medium sized dutch oven and pour in the coconut oil, then add onions and celery and cook for 3 minutes, then add garlic and cook for an additional one minute

Add the vinegar and stir until it evaporates

Stir in all the spices

Add the chopped cauliflower, salt, bay leaf, and water. Heat until it boils

Lower heat, cover, and simmer.

When the cauliflower is soft, remove bay leaf and stir to make the soup's texture more creamy, then serve

Dinner: Vegan Tofu Tacos

INGREDIENTS

1 cup of cooked black beans

8 ounces of firm tofu

Half a medium sized red onion, diced

1 cup fresh cilantro, chopped

1 or 2 sliced avocados

0.25 cup of pomegranate seeds

Half a cup of salsa

Corn tortillas

SEASONING FOR TOFU:

Half a teaspoon of chili powder

1 teaspoon of cumin

1 teaspoon of garlic powder

Pinch of ground course sea salt

1 tablespoon of salsa

1 tablespoon of water

INSTRUCTIONS

Wrap tofu in a clean, absorbent towel and place something heavy on top, such as a cast iron skillet, while prepping toppings.

Cook black beans according to instructions on package, add a pinch each of salt, chili powder, cumin, and garlic powder, then set aside

Add the tofu seasoning and salsa to a bowl and top with just enough water to make a sauce that can be poured, then set aside.

Heat a pan over medium heat and add 1-2 tablespoons of oil and chopped tofu. Cook for 5 minutes, stirring frequently, then add seasoning. Cook for another 8 minutes, still stirring frequently.

Warm the tortillas and fill them with all of the ingredients, then serve and enjoy!

Juice: Sourpuss Supreme

Three large stalks of celery
Three medium sized apples
One large orange, peeled
One thumbnail sized piece of ginger root
One lemon, unpeeled
One lime, unpeeled
Two cloves of garlic

Day 20

Breakfast: Creamy Cashew Parfait

INGREDIENTS

1 cup of muesli

1 cup of cashew nut cream

1 cup of mixed frozen berries (do not thaw)

Quarter of a cup of toasted almond flakes

Ground cinnamon (to taste)

INSTRUCTIONS

Simply combine the ingredients, stir, and serve!

Lunch: Quinoa Protein Power Patty

INGREDIENTS

1 cup quinoa, (make sure you wash thoroughly first!)

1 bunch of spring onions (dice the white portion)

1 cup of chopped kale

4 eggs, preferably from your local farmer's market

2 cloves of garlic, chopped

1 cup of your favorite fresh whole grain bread crumbs

Ground course sea salt, to taste

Ground pepper, to taste

INSTRUCTIONS

Cook your washed quinoa according to the instructions on the package. After it is cooked, let it cool.

Stir your eggs in a bowl.

Mix all the ingredients together, including eggs and quinoa, stirring thoroughly.

Heat a large frying pan over medium heat. Add some minimally processed oil such as coconut oil if you like.

Spoon a portion of the mixture into the pan, using a spatula to press it down into the shape of a patty.

Cook until the edges start to brown, then flip and cook the other side until the edges start to brown.

Serve alone or on a whole grain bun or pita

Dinner: Toasty Kale Pecan Squash

INGREDIENTS

1 medium sized butternut squash

3 garlic cloves, minced

4 tablespoons fresh parsley, chopped

Pinch of ground course sea salt (or to taste)

Half a tablespoon of extra virgin olive oil

1 cup of fresh chopped kale

ADDITIONAL INGREDIENTS TO BE PROCESSED:

1 tablespoon of nutritional yeast

0.25 cups of almonds

0.25 cups of pecans

1 teaspoon of extra virgin olive oil

Pinch of ground course sea salt

INSTRUCTIONS

Preheat oven to 400F/205C and lightly coat your casserole dish

with oil

Peel the squash, remove the top and bottom, then cut into two halves. Scoop out the guts and seeds. Further chop the two halves of squash into cubes of about 3 cm each and add the cubes to the casserole dish.

Add parsley, salt, minced garlic, and oil into the casserole dish and stir until well mixed with the squash cubes.

Cover and bake for 40-50 minutes.

While baking, combine the pecans, almonds, yeast, as well as a pinch of salt and 1 teaspoon of extra virgin olive oil in your food processor until chunky. Do not puree.

After 40-50 minutes, remove squash from the oven and turn off the heat. Add the chopped kale and sprinkle the mixture from the food processor all over the squash. Then return to the still hot oven for 10 5 minutes to warm the processed ingredients.

Serve and enjoy!

Juice: Simple Farmer

Three medium sized green apples
One medium sized cucumber
One large stalk of celery
One cup of parsley
One cup of spinach
One lime, peeled

Day 21

Breakfast: Oat Cranberry Smoothie

INGREDIENTS

1 quarter cup of cranberries (fresh or frozen)

2 tablespoons rolled oats

1 cup almond milk

Half a pear

Dash of cinnamon (to taste)

INSTRUCTIONS

Simply combine all of the ingredients in a blender and blend until smooth. Enjoy!

Lunch: Lively Pumpkin Seed Salad

INGREDIENTS

3 cups of your favorite lettuce leaves, mixed greens, or spinach
0.25 cups roasted pumpkin seeds
0.25 cups currants

Dressing: 1 tablespoon extra virgin olive oil mixed with 2 teaspoons balsamic vinegar

INSTRUCTIONS

Simply chop the lettuce, mix all ingredients and serve!

Dinner: Lemon Pepper Kale and Garlic Salmon

INGREDIENTS

1 salmon fillet

Half a bunch of fresh kale, chopped

1 red bell pepper, sliced

5 cloves of garlic, finely chopped

Juice from one medium sized freshly squeezed lemon

1-2 tablespoons of almond butter

Half a red onion, diced

3 tablespoons of lemon pepper (or to taste)

INSTRUCTIONS

In a non-stick pan, or a pan lightly coated extra virgin olive oil, fry the salmon fillet 3-5 minutes per side over medium heat. With one minute left of cooking, add half the finely chopped garlic and lemon juice to the pan, then spoon over salmon fillet when serving.

Melt the almond butter in a pan over medium-low heat and add onion and red bell pepper.

After 3 minutes, add the chopped kale and the other half of the

garlic. Sprinkle with lemon pepper.

Use tongs to turn and mix the kale with the other ingredients in the pan. Ensure the kale is heated evenly. Remove after only 2 minutes.

Serve and enjoy! For more lemon flavor, garnish the salmon fillet with a thin slice of lemon and sprinkle with lemon pepper.

Juice: Superhero's Secret

Three medium sized guava
One medium sized green bell pepper
One medium clementine, peeled
One medium sized apple, any variety
One lime, peeled

30 Day Whole Food Challenge

Day 22

Breakfast: Banana Quinoa

INGREDIENTS

1 cup cooked quinoa
1 cup almond milk
Handful of raisins
Dash of cinnamon (to taste)

INSTRUCTIONS

Use a small pan or pot and bring quinoa, milk, raisins, and cinnamon to a gentle boil. Once boiling, reduce the heat and simmer. Stir the mix frequently for about five minutes. You'll know it is done when about half the milk has been absorbed. Garnish with fresh slices of banana and serve.

Lunch: Smashed Garlic Pinto Bean Pita

INGREDIENTS

1 onion, chopped

2 cups dry pinto beans (make sure you rinse them well and check for rocks)

Handful of fresh jalapeno peppers, chopped

4 cloves garlic, smashed and minced

1 teaspoon black pepper

1 teaspoon chili pepper

Two tablespoons of cumin

6 cups of water or your favorite broth

INSTRUCTIONS

Combine all ingredients in slow cooker and cook on high for at least 6 hours (8 hours is best).

Drain any excess liquid. Serve in a bowl or in a warm, whole wheat pita.

Dinner: Fresh Snapper Ceviche

INGREDIENTS

Approximately 750g of fresh snapper, ensure all bones are removed and cut the meat into small cubes between 1 and 1.5 cm each

Juice from three fresh, medium sized limes

1.5 cups of coconut water

2 tablespoons of coriander leaves, chopped

2 tablespoons of mint leaves, chopped

4 spring onions, sliced fine

1 small red chili, sliced fine

Pinch of ground course sea salt

SALSA INGREDIENTS (if using as a dip)

1 ripe avocado, dice the flesh of the avocado into cubes of 1-2 cm each

1 red capsicum, diced

2 tablespoons chopped coriander

Juice from half a lime (lime zest to taste)

INSTRUCTIONS

Mix herbs, chili, lime juice, coconut water, and spring onions, in small bowl.

Add fish to mix and ensure all cubes are thoroughly coated.

Cover and refrigerate for 3-5 hours.

Garnish with additional coriander and mint to taste. Serve on it's own or as a dip with your favorite vegetables, or shrimp if you want additional protein.

Juice: ABC Juice (Asparagus, Broccoli, Cucumber)

One medium sized stalk of broccoli
One medium sized cucumber
Three large carrots
Two handfuls of parsley
Four stalks of celery
Four stalks of asparagus
Two medium sized green bell pepper

30 Day Whole Food Challenge

Day 23

Breakfast: Almond Raisin Oatmeal

INGREDIENTS

Steel cut oatmeal

Handful of raisins

Handful of almonds

Cinnamon

INSTRUCTIONS

Prepare the oatmeal according to the instructions on the package. When the oatmeal is halfway finished cooking, add the raisins and almonds. When finished cooking, add cinnamon to taste

Lunch: Shredded Yellow Curry Chicken Salad

INGREDIENTS

3 cups chicken, cooked and shredded

0.25 cups plain yogurt

1 teaspoon yellow curry powder

Handful of cilantro leaves, thoroughly washed

Handful of sliced almonds

INSTRUCTIONS

Simply combine the ingredients and toss for a delicious salad. If you'd like to add dressing, you can make your own simple, tasty, healthy dressing by combining 1 tablespoon of extra virgin olive oil mixed with 2 teaspoons of balsamic vinegar.

Dinner: Super Simple Chickpea Salad Pitas

INGREDIENTS

0.5 cups of chopped celery

1.5 cups of cooked chickpeas

1 medium sized dill pickle, chopped

1 garlic clove, minced

3 tablespoons of chopped red onion

1 tablespoon of fresh dill, minced

2 tablespoons of fresh lemon juice

0.5 cups of toasted sunflower seeds

Course ground sea salt and pepper to taste

INSTRUCTIONS

Preheat toaster oven to 325F/160C and toast your sunflower seeds for 8-10 minutes.

Mix all of the ingredients into a bowl

Spoon the mixture into some fresh whole wheat pitas and enjoy!

Juice: Pink Hijinx

One medium sized yam (sweet potato)
Two clementines, peeled
One beetroot
Two large carrots
One thumb-sized piece of ginger

Day 24

Breakfast: Baked Apple Pancakes

INGREDIENTS

2 Granny Smith apples, peeled and sliced paper thin

Approximately 4 tablespoons of almond butter, enough to cover your pan

3 eggs (preferably from a local farmer's market)

1 cup of coconut milk

2 teaspoons of cinnamon

3 tablespoons of coconut sugar (according to taste)

1 teaspoon of juice from freshly squeezed lemon

1 teaspoon of vanilla powder

half a teaspoon of sea salt

half a teaspoon of bicarbonate of soda

2 cups of almond meal

INSTRUCTIONS

Preheat oven to 180°C.

In an oven-proof pan melt the almond butter. It should coat the base of the pan completely

Cover the base of the pan in a single layer of apple slices. Sprinkle cinnamon and coconut sugar over the apple slices

In a blender or food processor, combine the eggs, milk, almond meal, remaining sugar, cinnamon, vanilla, sea salt, bicarbonate of soda. vinegar and mix until thoroughly combined.

Pour the mix over the apple slices.

Bake in your preheated oven for approximately 20 minutes or until the middle of the pancake is set

Lunch: Red Lentil Soup

INGREDIENTS

1 cup red lentils, washed thoroughly

3 celery stalks, chopped

1 large onion, chopped

2 large carrots, chopped

2 tablespoons of tomato paste

2 cups of broccoli florets

Pinch of oregano

1 bay leaf

6 leaves of basil, chopped

Pinch of ground thyme

5 cups water

INSTRUCTIONS

Simply combine ingredients in a slow cooker and cook for 4-5 hours on high. Enjoy!

Dinner: Rawlicious Spinach Stuffed Portobello Caps

INGREDIENTS

4 portobello mushroom caps

Juice three fresh medium sized lemons and zest one teaspoon (or to taste)

Half a cup of cashews

5 tablespoons of extra virgin olive oil

3 mined cloves of garlic

2 sliced scallions

Pinch of ground course sea salt (or to taste)

2 teaspoons of fresh rosemary, chopped

1 cup of spinach leaves

1 cup of corn kernels

INSTRUCTIONS

Combine and whisk oil, rosemary, garlic, salt, lemon juice and zest.

Place the mushroom caps, rounded side facing down, in a baking

dish. Gently pierce each cap several times with a fork or the tip of a knife.

Pour the mixture in equal portions in the mushroom caps, then cover and refrigerate between 3 and 8 hours.

Soak cashews in warm water for 20-40 minutes. Drain the water and process in your food processor with 0.25 cups of fresh water until you have a smooth puree. Add some ground course sea salt to taste.

Spoon the cashew puree into the mushroom caps. Garnish the mushroom caps with spinach, corn, scallions, and serve.

Juice: Cruciferous Craze

Eight leaves of kale
One cup of broccoli florets
One English cucumber
One medium sized green bell pepper
Two cups of spinach
One lemon, peeled

Day 25

Breakfast: Tasty and Healthy Whole Wheat Breakfast Crepes

INGREDIENTS

3 eggs (preferably from a local farmer's market)

1 cup whole-wheat flour

1 cup almond milk

1 teaspoon vanilla

A quarter of a teaspoon of salt

Half a cup of water

2 tablespoons of melted almond butter

INSTRUCTIONS

Put all of the ingredients in your blender and mix them thoroughly. Let the mix stand for 10 minutes.
Coat your frying pan with almond butter over medium heat.

Pour the batter on your pan held at an angle. Swirl the batter around to coat the entire the pan in one thin layer.

Push down the thin edges of the crepe around the perimeter using

a spatula.

After 45 seconds to 1 minute when the crepe is golden brown on the bottom, flip it over. Do this delicately to avoid ripping the crepe.

Cook another 45 seconds on the other side and then roll up each crepe.

Lunch: Kale Wrapped Navy Beans

INGREDIENTS

3 tbsp extra virgin olive oil

1 cup chopped onions

5 Cloves of garlic, minced

2-3 fresh whole tomatoes, blended

4 fresh basil leaves, chopped

Half teaspoon ground sage

2 cups cooked navy beans (cook for 6-8 hours in slow cooker)

INSTRUCTIONS

Add 3 tablespoons of olive oil and chopped onions to pot with lid and warm over low heat

Add garlic and saute until fragrant but not burnt.

Add tomatoes, sage, and basil leaves, stir and simmer for 5 minutes

Add cooked beans

Stir and simmer for 20 minutes

Spoon mix into leaves of kale, wrap and serve

Dinner: Mediterranean Quinoa Pitas

INGREDIENTS

0.5 cup quinoa, washed

1 medium sized chopped carrot

5 scallions, sliced thin

2 cups of any white beans (i.e. navy beans), as always ensure your beans are thoroughly washed and inspected for rocks

0.25 cups of whole grain bread crumbs

1 egg, preferably from your local farmers market

2 tablespoons extra virgin olive oil

Half an English cucumber, cut in diagonal thin slices

Ground coarse sea salt to taste

Dash of ground pepper, to taste

1 tablespoon ground cumin

0.5 cup of plain Greek yogurt

1 tablespoon fresh lemon juice

4 whole wheat pitas

INSTRUCTIONS

Cook quinoa according to instructions on package, then set aside.

Process carrot in your food processor until pieces are finely chopped, then add the cooked quinoa, egg, beans, breadcrumbs, cumin, 1 teaspoon of ground sea salt, a quarter of a teaspoon of pepper and half the scallions. Process until the ingredients are mixed, but still chunky.

Spoon the mixture into four patties, then refrigerate for 15 minutes to firm them up if necessary.

Heat oil in a pan over medium heat, then brown the patties, 6-8 minutes per side.

Mix lemon juice, Greek yogurt, and the other half of the scallions; season with ground coarse sea salt and pepper to taste.

Portion the mixture into the pitas, add one of the patties to each pita and serve.

Juice: Spinach Ginger Zing-a-linger

Two cups of spinach
Three leaves of kale
Four medium sized stalks of celery
One lemon, peeled
One lime, peeled
Three thumbnail sized pieces of ginger
Four cloves of garlic
Pinch of cayenne pepper (add after juicing)

30 Day Whole Food Challenge

Day 26

Breakfast: Spinach Omelet and Avocado

INGREDIENTS

2 eggs (best if you can purchase them from a local farmer's market)

2 Avocados

Handful of organic spinach

Big pinch of parsley

INSTRUCTIONS

Mix the yolks and egg whites in a bowl (or discard the yolks if you prefer). Pour eggs into a frying pan, top with spinach leaves and parsley. Slice both avocados in half and serve.

Lunch: Perfect Pesto Pasta

INGREDIENTS

Two cups of fresh sweet peas, cooked

1/2 cup extra virgin olive oil

1 handful of fresh basil

3 cloves of garlic, minced

Quarter cup pine nuts

Half teaspoon tsp onion powder

Half teaspoon garlic powder

Quarter cup red onion, finely diced

Handful of fresh cherry tomatoes

Pinch of sea salt

Your favorite pasta

INSTRUCTIONS

Mix the cooked sweet peas, basil, pine nuts, olive oil, garlic, onion powder and garlic powder in your blender.

Heat one tablespoon of extra virgin olive oil in a pan over

medium heat. Add diced onion to the pan.

After cooking for five minutes, add the cooked onion to the blender and blend.

Cook your pasta, then simply add your pesto from the blender to the cooked pasta, garnish with cherry tomatoes, toss thoroughly, and serve.

Dinner: South of the Border Spicy Pinto Beans

INGREDIENTS

1 pound pinto beans, washed and inspected for rocks

2 cups of fresh diced tomatoes

6 diced green chili peppers

1 large chopped yellow onion

1 1/2 teaspoons garlic powder

1 tablespoon ground cumin

1 tablespoon chili powder

INSTRUCTIONS

Soak beans overnight in a bowl of water, fully immersed

Place the drained beans in your crock pot, add fresh water such that all the beans are immersed, then add the onion, tomatoes, cumin, chili powder, and garlic powder.

Cook on high for 7-8 hours

Serve alone or in a whole wheat pita

Juice: Pepper and Cabbage

One quarter of a small head of green cabbage
One medium sized green bell pepper
One medium sized red bell pepper
One cup of spinach
One thumb sized piece of ginger root
Two medium sized carrots
One stalk of celery
Half a lemon, peeled

30 Day Whole Food Challenge

Day 27

Breakfast: Raspberry Chia Seed Pudding

INGREDIENTS

1.5 cups fresh or frozen raspberries (if frozen, thaw overnight in the fridge)

1.5 cups of coconut milk

0.5 cups of chia seeds

1 teaspoon of vanilla powder

0.25 cups of brown rice syrup (according to taste)

INSTRUCTIONS

Mix all ingredients thoroughly in a blender

Refrigerate overnight to allow the mix to thicken

Consume in the morning for a fast, simple, delicious, and healthy breakfast!

Lunch: Sweet Potato Powerhouse Mash

INGREDIENTS

1 sweet potato (wash but don't peel)

1 teaspoon of coconut oil

1 tablespoon of almond butter

Ground course sea salt and freshly ground black pepper, to taste

INSTRUCTIONS

Preheat oven to 200°C/400°F

Using a fork, puncture the sweet potato 4 to 5 times to prevent it from exploding.

Bake on a tray for approximately 30 minutes. It is done when you can easily slide a fork into and out of the sweet potato

Remove from oven (be careful it will be very hot!) then cut and scoop out the flesh into a bowl. Add the coconut oil and almond butter, season with the salt and pepper, mash, and serve.

Dinner: Cracked Pepper Quinoa Salmon Cakes

INGREDIENTS

2 cups of fresh salmon, cooked and chopped into cubes of 1-2cm each

1 egg, preferably from you local farmer's market

Half a cup of quinoa flakes (or substitute for any variety of fast cooking oats)

1 tablespoon low sodium soy sauce

2 cloves of garlic, minced

0.25 cups of fresh chopped parsley

2 teaspoons of freshly ground pepper, or to taste

1 tablespoon extra virgin coconut oil

2 green onions, thinly sliced

INSTRUCTIONS

Combine all ingredients other than the oil and mix in a bowl

Spoon the mixture into patties (makes 6-8 patties)

Pour the oil in a medium sized pan and heat over medium-low heat.

Cook the salmon patties until golden brown, approximately 4 minutes per side.

Serve alone or in a warmed whole wheat pita with chopped romaine lettuce.

Juice: Mister Cruciferous

Three cups of broccoli florets
Four leaves of kale
One large orange, peeled
One English cucumber
One lemon, peeled
One lime, peeled

30 Day Whole Food Challenge

Day 28

Breakfast: Oat Cranberry Smoothie

INGREDIENTS

1 quarter cup of cranberries (fresh or frozen)

2 tablespoons rolled oats

1 cup almond milk

Half a pear

Dash of cinnamon (to taste)

INSTRUCTIONS

Simply combine all of the ingredients in a blender and blend until smooth. Enjoy!

Lunch: Healthy High Fiber Hummus

INGREDIENTS

1.5 cups of chickpeas (washed)

4 tablespoons of hulled tahini

1 clove of garlic, diced

Juice from one medium sized lemon

1 teaspoon cumin powder

Half a teaspoon of cinnamon powder

2 tablespoons of water

2 tablespoons of extra virgin olive oil

One pinch of ground course sea salt, or to taste

Black pepper to taste

INSTRUCTIONS

Simply use a food processor to thoroughly process all of the
ingredients, then serve

Dinner: Vegan Chickpea Salad

INGREDIENTS

3 cups cooked chickpeas

Half a cup of chopped sun dried tomatoes

3 tablespoons fresh squeezed lemon juice

15 fresh basil leaves, chopped

1 tablespoon of apple cider vinegar

2 tablespoons of extra virgin olive oil

Pinch of fresh ground pepper, to taste

INSTRUCTIONS

Blanch your sun dried tomatoes by placing them in a small bowl and pouring boiling fresh water over them, and soaking them for 5 minutes.

Drain the bowl, then slice the sun dried tomatoes.

Combine all ingredients including the sun dried tomatoes, serve and enjoy!

Juice: Mighty Toxin Slayer

Two medium sized green bell pepper
One medium sized cucumber
One large stalk of celery
One cup of parsley
One cup of spinach
One lime, peeled

Day 29

Breakfast: Banana Quinoa

INGREDIENTS

1 cup cooked quinoa
1 cup almond milk
Handful of raisins
Dash of cinnamon (to taste)

INSTRUCTIONS

Use a small pan or pot and bring quinoa, milk, raisins, and cinnamon to a gentle boil. Once boiling, reduce the heat and simmer. Stir the mix frequently for about five minutes. You'll know it is done when about half the milk has been absorbed. Garnish with fresh slices of banana and serve.

Lunch: Quinoa Protein Power Patty

INGREDIENTS

1 cup quinoa, (make sure you wash thoroughly first!)

1 bunch of spring onions (dice the white portion)

1 cup of chopped kale

4 eggs, preferably from your local farmer's market

2 cloves of garlic, chopped

1 cup of your favorite fresh whole grain bread crumbs

Ground course sea salt, to taste

Ground pepper, to taste

INSTRUCTIONS

Cook your washed quinoa according to the instructions on the package. After it is cooked, let it cool.

Stir your eggs in a bowl.

Mix all the ingredients together, including eggs and quinoa, stirring thoroughly.

Heat a large frying pan over medium heat. Add some minimally processed oil such as coconut oil if you like.

Spoon a portion of the mixture into the pan, using a spatula to press it down into the shape of a patty.

Cook until the edges start to brown, then flip and cook the other side until the edges start to brown.

Serve alone or on a whole grain bun or pita

Dinner: Toasty Kale Pecan Squash

INGREDIENTS

1 medium sized butternut squash

3 garlic cloves, minced

4 tablespoons fresh parsley, chopped

Pinch of ground course sea salt (or to taste)

Half a tablespoon of extra virgin olive oil

1 cup of fresh chopped kale

ADDITIONAL INGREDIENTS TO BE PROCESSED:

1 tablespoon of nutritional yeast

0.25 cups of almonds

0.25 cups of pecans

1 teaspoon of extra virgin olive oil

Pinch of ground course sea salt

INSTRUCTIONS

Preheat oven to 400F/205C and lightly coat your casserole dish

with oil

Peel the squash, remove the top and bottom, then cut into two halves. Scoop out the guts and seeds. Further chop the two halves of squash into cubes of about 3 cm each and add the cubes to the casserole dish.

Add parsley, salt, minced garlic, and oil into the casserole dish and stir until well mixed with the squash cubes.

Cover and bake for 40-50 minutes.

While baking, combine the pecans, almonds, yeast, as well as a pinch of salt and 1 teaspoon of extra virgin olive oil in your food processor until chunky. Do not puree.

After 40-50 minutes, remove squash from the oven and turn off the heat. Add the chopped kale and sprinkle the mixture from the food processor all over the squash. Then return to the still hot oven for 10 5 minutes to warm the processed ingredients.

Serve and enjoy!

Juice: The Scale Loves Kale

Four stalks of celery
Six kale leaves
Three apples, any variety
Three cloves of garlic
One lime, peeled
Half of one lemon, peeled

Day 30

Breakfast: Almond Raisin Oatmeal

INGREDIENTS

Steel cut oatmeal

Handful of raisins

Handful of almonds

Cinnamon

INSTRUCTIONS

Prepare the oatmeal according to the instructions on the package. When the oatmeal is halfway finished cooking, add the raisins and almonds. When finished cooking, add cinnamon to taste.

Lunch: Healthy High Fiber Hummus

INGREDIENTS

1.5 cups of chickpeas (washed)

4 tablespoons of hulled tahini

1 clove of garlic, diced

Juice from one medium sized lemon

1 teaspoon cumin powder

Half a teaspoon of cinnamon powder

2 tablespoons of water

2 tablespoons of extra virgin olive oil

One pinch of ground course sea salt, or to taste

Black pepper to taste

INSTRUCTIONS

Simply use a food processor to thoroughly process all of the ingredients, then serve.

Dinner: Vegan Tofu Tacos

INGREDIENTS

1 cup of cooked black beans

8 ounces of firm tofu

Half a medium sized red onion, diced

1 cup fresh cilantro, chopped

1 or 2 sliced avocados

0.25 cup of pomegranate seeds

Half a cup of salsa

Corn tortillas

SEASONING FOR TOFU:

Half a teaspoon of chili powder

1 teaspoon of cumin

1 teaspoon of garlic powder

Pinch of ground course sea salt

1 tablespoon of salsa

1 tablespoon of water

INSTRUCTIONS

Wrap tofu in a clean, absorbent towel and place something heavy on top, such as a cast iron skillet, while prepping toppings.

Cook black beans according to instructions on package, add a pinch each of salt, chili powder, cumin, and garlic powder, then set aside

Add the tofu seasoning and salsa to a bowl and top with just enough water to make a sauce that can be poured, then set aside.

Heat a pan over medium heat and add 1-2 tablespoons of oil and chopped tofu. Cook for 5 minutes, stirring frequently, then add seasoning. Cook for another 8 minutes, still stirring frequently.

Warm the tortillas and fill them with all of the ingredients, then serve and enjoy!

Juice: Sprout Celebration

Six Brussels sprouts
Two beetroot
Three large carrots
One third of a medium sized pineapple

30 Day Whole Food Challenge

Conclusion

Congratulations on completing the 30 day whole food challenge. Think back to a month ago and recall the state of your health at that time. I'd be willing to bet you lost fat and gained energy – probably a lot – over the last 30 days.

Your 30 day challenge is now complete, but you're only at the beginning of your journey to living a maximally healthy lifestyle. Having seen the difference a clean and healthy diet can make, I'm sure you have no desire to go back to eating processed, calorie-dense, nutrient deficient foods that so many people are slowly killing themselves with in our modern food dystopia. Turn your 30 day challenge into a year long challenge. Then a decade long challenge. Then a lifetime challenge. Enjoy all the benefits that come with making the whole food diet a whole food lifestyle.

One Final Thing...

I really hope you've been enjoying the recipes in this book and that they've helped you to energize and reach your health and weight loss goals. I would love to hear from you! If you enjoyed reading this book I would be extremely grateful if you could take just one minute of your time and write a review online on Amazon or on social media. I personally read all my Amazon reviews and they help me to make my future books even better. Thank you so much for your support, it means the world to me!

Yours in healthy living,

Albert Pino

30 Day Whole Food Challenge

Sign up to get healthy living tips and tricks as well as a free bonus ebook at:

www.albertpino.com

52541106R00117

Made in the USA
Lexington, KY
01 June 2016